# Contents

# Chapter One

# Introduction

Many readers will be familiar with operational schemes[1] which were first identified by Athey in her 1990 publication; 'Extending Thought in Young Children'. These schemes include 'transporting', 'rotating', 'ordering', 'dabbing' and many more. Schemes are all common behaviours that have been observed in the play of many children between the ages of two and four. 'Good practice' suggests that we should observe and identify any particular scheme that a child is displaying and then provide the resources and environment to allow the scheme to extend into other contexts. For example, identification of a child transporting objects around the early years' setting using a basket, can be built upon and extended by the educator through the provision of other means of transportation, such as a wheel barrow, or a shopping trolley. Another example might be an educator noticing a child turning on and off taps that twist or playing with spinning tops and extending his or her interest by providing further resources such as a water wheel or objects that roll or rotate. The provision of new resources enable the child to consolidate an existing scheme, and apply it to new contexts.

Having reviewed Chris Athey's data files at the Froebel archive, we came to realise, as she clearly did, that EVERY behaviour we observe children repeatedly applying is a scheme, and the reason that children are seen to repeat them is almost certainly because of the novelty and fun of having discovered them. These schemes repeated in play extend and continue to be observed in many children at least until the age of 6 or 7 years.

Following our observations and engagements with practitioners, in a variety of early years' contexts, we have come to realise that the schemes that are currently identified in the early years' educational literature provide just the tip of the learning 'iceberg'!

---

[1] Referred sometimes as *schemas* see p8 below.

We have also come to realise, again as Athey did herself, that many of the schemes are of crucial importance in the development of literacy and numeracy. We now realise that further knowledge of these behaviours can be enormously helpful in supporting children's learning and development, and enable more children to reach the learning outcomes as identified in the Early Learning Goals (DfE, 2013).

## So what is the role of the educator?

The role of the educator in support of learning through play is firstly to ensure that a stimulating play environment for the child is created, where they have total freedom to choose their activity. If we are to encourage schematic play, the child's independence is critical; they need to be able to access their play materials freely and return them to their proper place when they have finished with them. When a child knows where to find the materials they require for a particular activity they are more likely to use them repeatedly in their play, and it is in the repetition of the schemes that they consolidate their newly acquired skills and understandings. It is at this point that we can also provide new material challenges within their play theme and extend these schemes to be applied in new contexts.

Repetition is key for skills to develop; we readily appreciate this when we consider learning how to play a new musical instrument, but is not always valued in children's play activity as a facilitator for learning and development.

When a child is free to repeat an activity for as long as s/he chooses, the educator's observations provides a reliable and useful picture of what a child 'can do' and what they 'know'. The educator can then provide the most appropriate resources, and emotional scaffolding to effectively support the child's learning further. We refer to this later in our writing as 'seeding' the play learning environment.

Children's schemes should also be built upon, just like building blocks. For example, if we consider the scheme of addition, it is built up from a combination of schemes that include one to one correspondence, matching, seriation, sequencing, ordering, grading, visual discrimination. Each of these can be supported to encourage a knowledge and understanding of measuring and other mathematical concepts (See Chapter 4).

Children need as much independent control of their time as possible, especially if they are going to be supported to become fully immersed and engaged in their play and learning. Unfortunately, in many preschool settings, bells may be routinely rung, interrupting their play, in order to gain their attention; 'tidy up time' songs may be sung in the middle of a morning session, in some cases these interruptions' become a part and parcel of the background hum and become meaningless to the children. Children may also be too often required to sit on a carpet or mat whilst educators organise group activities: But perhaps we should question and reflect, *"Does this really support the child's full immersion in their play, does it really enable and create a joy of learning?"*

*"Are we unintentionally losing just that individual child centred involvement and engagement in learning that we want to encourage?"*

There are strategies that we can employ to reduce these distractions. If children learn to return their play resources on every occasion, then 'tidy up time' isn't required. If children learn to prepare their own snacks and drinks they can be doing this when convenient to them rather than to the adults.

## Does the adult sometimes get in the way?

It is never the intention of anyone working with young children to be an obstacle to their learning and development, and it can feel uncomfortable to consider the adult in the early years setting in these terms. But the fact is that adults can sometimes distract the child from their playful learning, and adults are always a potential distraction to children's play, just by being in the room! There are some key points that are worth reflecting upon in your practice:

* When children arrive at the early years' setting can they find the activities that they were introduced to the day before, so that they can revisit them, continue an interest and use it for as long as they wish?
* Can they continue to develop an activity over a period of days? For example, place a name card on their construction and return to it the next day?
* Are children who are totally immersed in their play sometimes being asked to stop and put their activity away for no good purpose?
* Are activities self-contained so that they can be accessed independently, i.e. in a basket or some form of container which is easily carried to a table or floor space; i.e. positively promoting its use?
* When a child is engaged, are the adults sometimes disturbing them?
* Is the educators' involvement reducing children's independent and active engagement, i.e. do some adults feel that in order to be seen to be doing a good job, there is a need to engage with children at all times, possibly interrupting a child's 'flow' with questions such as "What are you making?"

Please do not misinterpret this last point: Of course, there are times when open questions and extended dialogues are valuable, but consider how these might be more usefully applied, such as when a child remarks on what they have made, or asks for advice.

In order for children to truly immerse themselves in play and learning, they

need the freedom to choose and repeat activities and, most importantly, the time and space to do so.

Concerns about finding the balance between teaching and play are addressed in the next chapter in which we begin

with an introduction to the theory and rationale of 'free flow play'. Most of the theoretical ideas that will be presented are widely accepted and promoted by early childhood academics, and they are backed up by strong empirical evidence. The novelty in our approach should be recognised as much less the result of any special selection or identification of the theoretical principles themselves, but rather in the way that we have chosen to combine and present them.

Developmental psychology, just like every other scientific discipline, provides theoretical models that are intended to help us understand our observations. They may be considered more or less to approximate or represent reality, but their value is most significantly in their pragmatic usefulness in allowing us to make predictions and carry out our work more effectively. In this particular case our model has been developed with the intention of improving our educational practice. To this end, in the following we provide a summary account of the cognitive processes of learning. We introduce key terms that describe what is involved, and we apply these to explain why it is that free flow play actually 'works' in practice, and what role there is for adult educators and carers in supporting it. In chapter three we will be; 'Putting the Schema back into Schema Theory and Practice', and then in our final chapter we explain how emergent literacy works with; *Emergence and the EYFS* [DfE, 2014] *curriculum.*

# Chapter Two

# Explaining Free Flow Play

In this chapter, we provide an introduction to the theory and rationale of 'free flow play'. To begin at the beginning with child development and learning, it is important at first to consider how we come to acquire and apply a knowledge of the world around us. One of the most common assumptions is that we come to hold in our minds some figurative form of representation of the objects around us. Since Piaget, developmental psychologists have commonly referred to these figurative representations as 'Schemas'. The simplest form of learning provides a one-to-one correspondence between some particular object or stimulus and its visual schema representation in the mind. Piaget (1969) referred to such learning as 'reproductive' and Vygotsky (1962) as 'empirical', and then moved their attention on to consider the much more interesting and challenging subject of conceptual learning. Whilst Piaget and Vygotsky are often presented as offering entirely alternative accounts of child development, in this and in many other respects their work can be seen as consistent and complimentary.

To take a simple example of a concept, we can consider the case of flowers. At an early stage of our learning about flowers we may have seen roses, lilies and/or other varieties and used a single image and/or the word flower in our mind to represent them. We might also use the word flower, and the name of a particular flower such as a rose interchangeably, but at some point in our social and cultural interactions we will be encouraged to differentiate between different flowers, to note particular characteristics and to recognise that the word 'flower' provides an abstract higher order category or 'concept' that includes all of those particular varieties that we have learnt about. Our life experiences, conversations and observations of other people around us will then lead us to elaborate upon this structure of representations in our mind. New varieties will be added to the structure such as the blossom that we see on trees, and we may learn that flowers support the reproduction of plants, that they are brightly coloured to attract insects who help the plant in dispersing its seeds. Connections will therefore be made to other concepts that we have developed, and we may add cognitive representations of different parts of the flower, of petals, stamens, pollen, etc. A good way of imagining this emerging cognitive structure is in terms of a 'mind map' which can become extremely complex and elaborate when we take a special interest and study any subject in depth. We illustrate this opposite with part of the schematic 'mind map' of an academic Botanist.

In his later work, Piaget (1969) made a distinction between the cognitive 'schemes' that provide the child with a knowledge and recall of physical actions (operations), and children's figurative visual 'schemas' as described above:

"The terms 'scheme' and 'schema' correspond to quite distinct realities, the one operative [a scheme of action in the sense of an instrument of generalization] and the other figurative" (Piaget, 1969, p ix).

Piaget came to believe that learning involved a progressive cyclical process in the development of these figurative 'schema', and their operative 'schemes'. As a child encounters each new experience, s/he refers at first to their prior knowledge to make sense of what an object 'does' and then what an object 'is'. Athey was aware of the distinction between schemes and schemas and acknowledged that:

"If more were known about the build-up of coordinated schemas [schemes] and concepts [schemas] more would be known about how best to teach some of the key concepts of the curriculum right through schooling" (Athey, 2007, p114).

A significant contribution towards clarifying this distinction between schemes and schemas was also made by Gibson (1969) who argued that we only perceive objects or events through their 'affordances'; or what we can 'do' with them.

A child may have a figurative scheme for an aeroplane, but it is only when the child perceives what an aeroplane does that it is possible for them to differentiate it from other objects, such as a car or a truck.

10

# The 'mind map' of an academic Botanist.

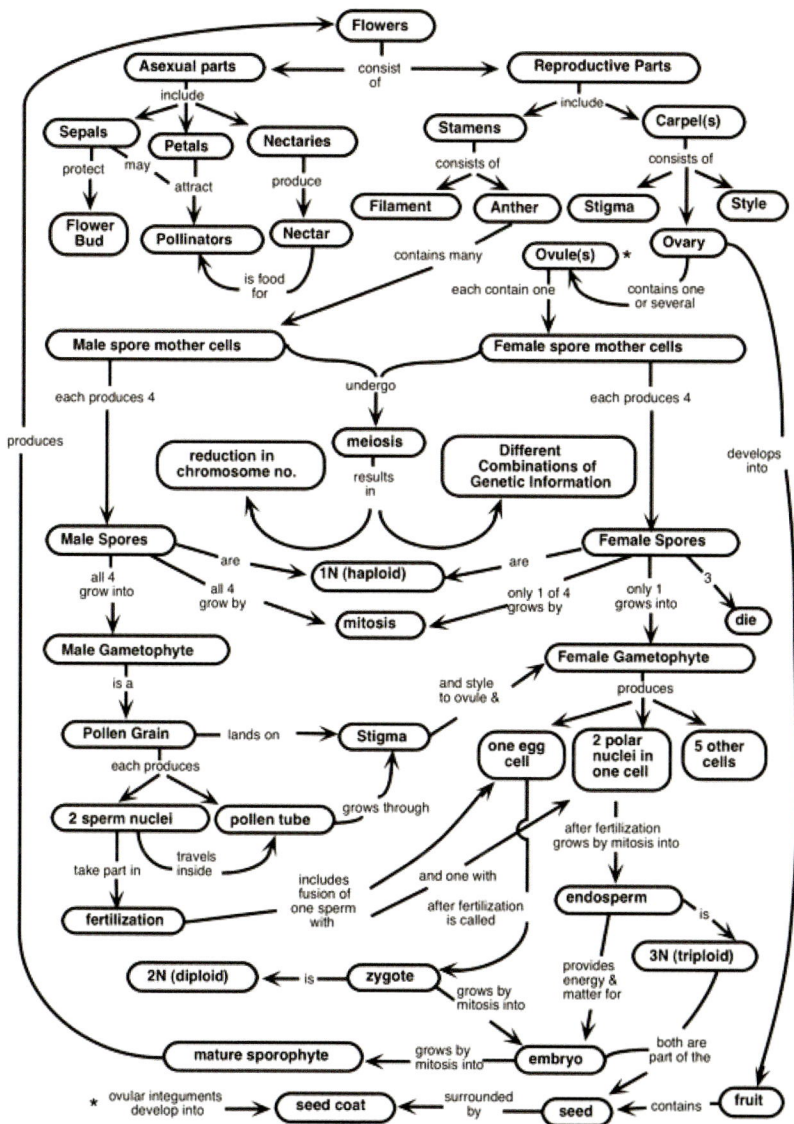

Operative Schemes are therefore increasingly considered fundamental to perception and an increasing number of theorists are referring to a new paradigm of 'embodied cognition'. Eleanor Gibson (1969) referred in her work to an 'ecological theory of child development'.

Perhaps surprisingly, as far as we are aware, our research represents the very first application of these ideas to early childhood education. New evidence supporting the use of the distinction between schemes and schema has also recently come from Neuroscience, as noted in the findings of the Cambridge Primary Review of research evidence (Alexander et al, 2010):

"Piaget's recognition that children actively construct their knowledge of the world through their action upon it has been upheld. As Goswami and Bryant explain, the discovery of 'mirror neurons' (brain cells which fire both when a person performs an action and when they observe someone else performing it) indicates that sensorimotor knowledge is the starting point of cognitive development, but that it is augmented rather than replaced by symbolic representations 'gained through action, language, pretend play and teaching'" (p91).

'Schema practice', has been considered to involve the practitioner in first identifying and then encouraging the child's 'patterns of repeated behaviour' into which new experiences are then 'assimilated and gradually co-ordinated' (Athey, 1990, p37). But, as Athey argued herself, research progress has been hindered by the ambiguity in the use of the terms and the fundamental difference between operative and figurative thinking has been 'worthy of further study' (*op cit*, p113-14) for many years. It has been for all these reasons that we have consistently applied the terms scheme to denote operative, and schema to denote figurative knowledge throughout this text.

## Applying schemes and schemas to explain Free Flow Play

Laevers' (1993) has applied Csikszentmihalyi's (1979, 1990) concept of flow in describing the complete immersion, involvement and sense of fulfilment of young children engaged in free play. As Bruce (2004) puts it, free flow play provides opportunities for children to 'try out their most recently acquired skills and competences, as if celebrating what they know' (p132). In cognitive terms, this is precisely what the child is doing, they are playfully 'trying on', just for the fun of it, different schemas to see how they fit (or not) to different schemes, and they are trying out different schemes to see how they work (or not) with different schemas. This is a powerful process in cognitive development described by Piaget as assimilation, and it is all about making connections in the mind, it is about fitting schemes and schemas together. Whilst we might consider the question of which comes first, an example of the 'chicken and egg' paradox, play clearly does require some prior knowledge acquisition, what Piaget referred to as schematic 'accommodation'. As Furth (1969) has explained:

"The child who re-enacts a scene from yesterday represents through symbol formation the event which was yesterday present to him through object formation…It gives food to his growing operative thinking which otherwise would be limited to perceptual events of here and now." (Furth, 1969, p89)

Free flow play may be considered 'seeded' by the child's prior learning of a scheme or schema. This may have occurred through the child's observation and imitation of others or through direct instruction, but it is important to recognise that the child's learning will remain incomplete if they are not provided with the opportunity to play with the new ideas, to identify the strengths and limitations of the schemes and schemas, and to own them for themselves. This is what we mean when we say that learning is essentially a creative and child centred process.

Elizabeth had been involved in a project growing hyacinths for sale to parents. In her free flow play she later created her own shop.

As Vygotsky noted, what we are supporting through play are the development of skills and understandings that are still in an embryonic state:

"These functions could be termed the 'buds' or 'flowers' of development rather than the 'fruits' of development" (Vygotsky, 1978, p. 42).

The following diagram represents the cognitive processes involved, described by van Oers (1999), as a process of 'progressive continuous re-contextualisation', where:

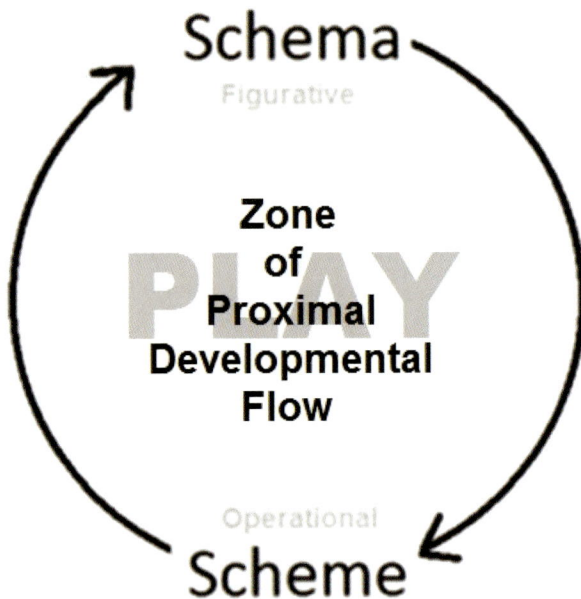

"A child's play is not simply a reproduction of what he has experienced, but a creative reworking of the impressions he has acquired" (Vygotsky, 1987, p11).

As Laevers (1993) observed, the child's total involvement, or immersion, can only occur within the zone of activity that matches the child's capabilities.

Vygotsky, (1962) referred to this as their 'zone of proximal development' (ZPD). In free flow play, the child is scaffolding their own learning through the recall of existing schemes and schema and we therefore refer to this as play within the Zone of Proximal Developmental Flow (ZPDF).

In the complete SchemaPlay model below, the adult's role, is represented in the outer cycle (top left). The adult will draw upon their knowledge of appropriate schemas and schemes, sensitively selecting appropriate focused activities to 'seed' the child's playful learning.

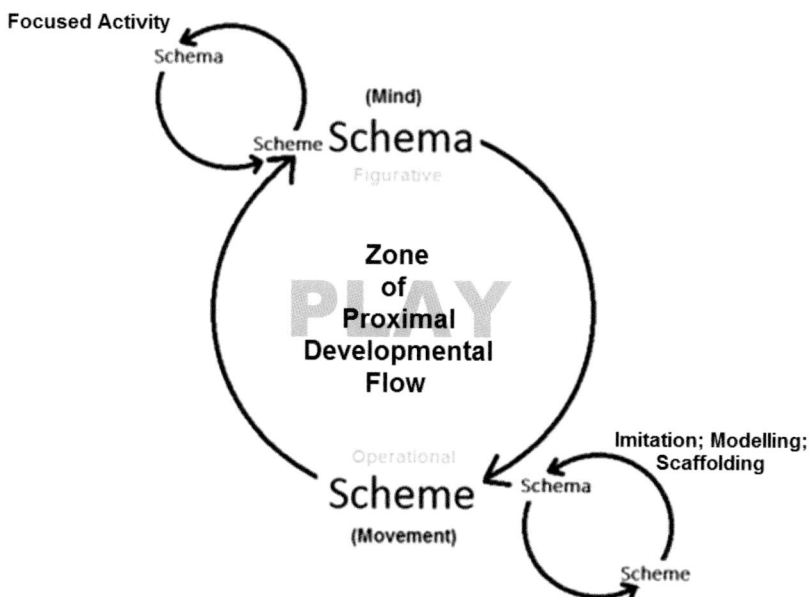

The adult's role, is therefore to provide at times the schematic resources for the child to play with. These activities may sometimes be systematically applied, as in the case of Montessori presentations, or much less formally in providing curriculum focused activities for an individual child or a small group. The relative size of the schema-scheme cycles provides an indication of their relative weighting. At the induction stage, where children are new to the preschool, they will require more support but, in a typical week, it is unlikely that a child aged 3 or 4 would benefit from more than two or three short  focused activities. The adult also has a role in providing the opportunities for the child to learn from others, and to support and encourage the child to continue playing within their zone of proximal developmental flow.

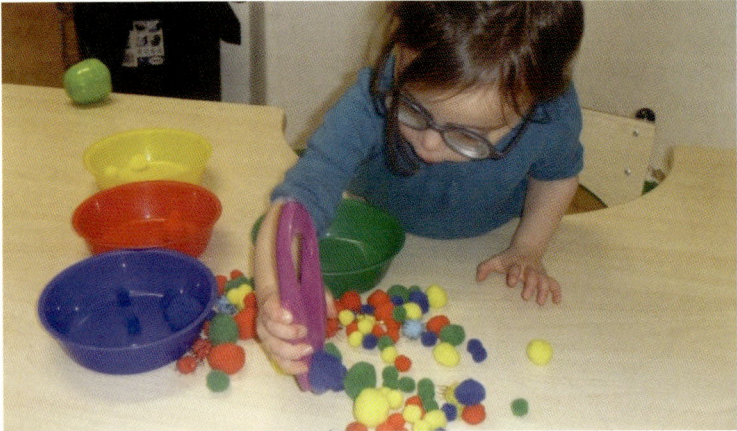

To give a practical example, Helen was observed using many colours in her painting and drawing.  Her Mother had also expressed some concern about the difficulties she seemed to be experiencing holding a crayon.  Her educator therefore provided a colour sorting activity to build on her interest in colour and encouraged her to use tongs in the process to support her pincer grip.

Helen was later observed sorting other coloured objects and materials and she encouraged other children to join this activity.

Helen's educator followed this up a week later by providing her with colour paint swatches to vishually discriminate grade by shade.

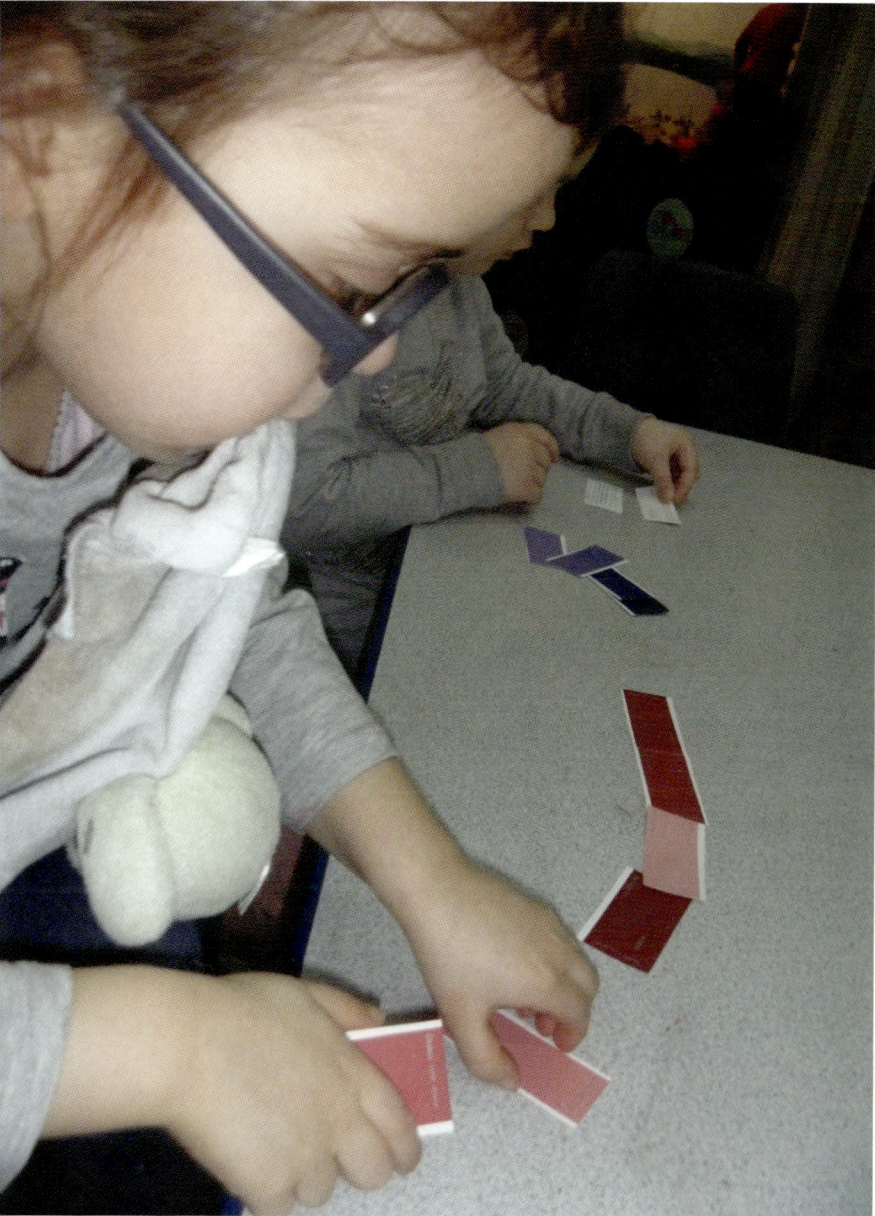

Soon after this Helen was engaged in painting and asked her educator for some help:

*"I want to make the brown darker Andrea; how can I make the brown darker? It is too light."*

This led to her be shown how to add some black paint to the brown she had and to subsequent paint mixing activities.

# Chapter Three

# Schema Theory and Practice

The essence of Piaget's concept of sensory motor intelligence is that infants construct their knowledge of the world from motor activity. As Fagard and Wolff (1991) have put it, "Mental representations (ideas, plans, images, thoughts) are internalised motor activity" (p179). Whilst Piaget developed his model primarily from the perspective of the child's earliest development, all of this may be considered consistent with Vygotsky's notion of the tools of intellectual adaptation that are gained from the surrounding culture. For Vygotsky, child development was considered to involve a progressive internalisation of, and adaptation to, the culture that is achieved later primarily through language (Rogoff, 1990). The implications of this for education are, as Bodrova and Leong (2007) have noted:

"... the tools are learned from adults and suggest that the role of the teacher is to 'arm children' with these tools. This sounds simple, but the process involves more than merely direct teaching of facts and skills. It involves enabling the child to use the tools independently and creatively. As children grow and develop, they become active tool users and tool makers; they become crafters. Eventually, they will be able to use mental tools appropriately and invent new tools when necessary"( Bodrova and Leong, 2007 p4.).

In a 2015 TACTYC research brief we reported on an activity carried out in a Montessori preschool setting involving 'Jack' (Siraj-Blatchford and Brock, 2016). Jack was at first observed grading and constructing towers with wooden blocks. His educator extended his grading scheme by introducing him to a grading activity involving the use of Montessori 'Red Rods' as pictured below.

In grading the red rods, Jack learnt to discriminate lengths and he applied his length schema in a variety of free flow play contexts. In one case he led a group of children in measuring the sticks they required to build a den.

## Montessori 'Red Rods'

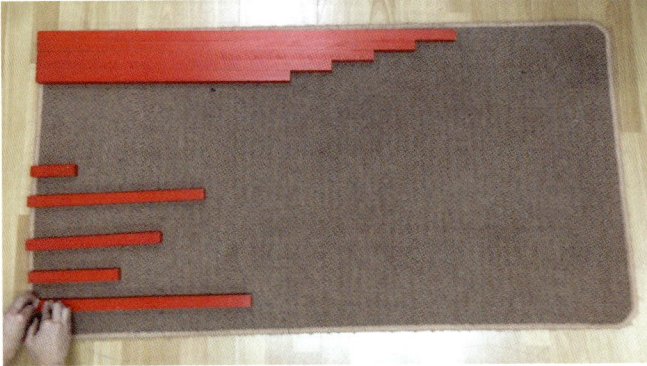

## Jack's 'Den'

Following Neisser (1976) and Anderson and Spiro (1977), we may identify the following as the main characteristics of mental 'schema' as they have come to be generally understood:

* they are organised in the mind in a meaningful way;
* they are embedded within superordinate and subordinate schemata;
* different schema may be applied in the course of an interaction with the environment;
* schema are reorganised when they commonly or calamitously fail to be useful; and
* they are more than the sum of their parts; they tend to reify and bias our perceptions (they are emergent mental representations).

In Chapter four we explain how emergent literacy and other 'emergent' concepts and cognitive operations are developed through schemes. Athey (1990) hoped that providing educators with knowledge of 'schemes' might help them to meet the needs, and support children's learning more appropriately. As Nutbrown (2006, p20) has argued, there is good supportive evidence of the benefits of this work, as a knowledge of schemes is helpful to practitioners in terms of their:

"…observations, planning, teaching, assessment, record-keeping and reflection … [and enable educators to] … create situations which challenge young children, enable 'fine tuning' of thinking and action, and ensure equality of access and curriculum."

To illustrate the benefits of identifying schemes and schemas in practice, we can take the examples of Fiona and Flora, two three year olds attending a large town centre pre-school in Kent.

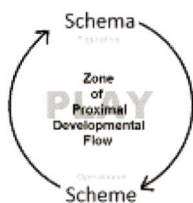

**Flora (3:9)** was observed engaged in free-flow play early in November 2016. She was sitting next to her friend and announced, "I am writing a letter, a letter to my Mummy – look!" Flora held up her mark making and smiled. Her key person, decided that a variety of both indoor and outdoor resources should be provided to encourage more mark-making and to reinforce the idea that text carries meaning. As Flora had been 'writing a letter', the role-play 'post office' in the garden was introduced to her and a variety of marking making tools provided. It was also

21

agreed that Flora's play should be closely observed over the following days to identify whether the horizontal and vertical trajectory schemes were being applied in any other play contexts.

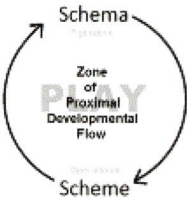

The following week, Flora was observed walking over to the book corner. She selected a book which she took over to a rug where she sat down. She then opened it and placed two fingers under the text moving them horizontally from left to right, as though reading! She did not say anything as she did this but, as she came to the last word on the page, she looked up and called out to her key person:

*"Can you come and look at this?"* She then asked, *"Are any of these letters in my name?"*

Flora was applying a horizontal trajectory scheme, she was also demonstrating her capability of applying one-to-one correspondence and her understanding that the text carried meaning.

After her key person had identified the letters from her name for her, Flora took the book back to the book corner and announced:

*"I am going to write a letter now"*

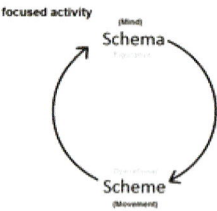

Given Flora's use of the horizontal and vertical trajectories and her interest in letters, a focussed activity was provided: Flora was supported in cutting each of the letters of her name out of light card; f/l/o/r/a. She then coated each of them with glue which she sprinkled with sand. Once they were dry her key person showed Flora how to trace her finger along each of the letter shapes in an anticlockwise direction and to voice the individual phonic sounds of each letter. Sand is used on the letters in this activity to add a tactile dimension and to support the child's recall of the letter shape.

22

Later Flora showed her Mother the letters drying on a rack:

"Mummy, I made letters in my name today. Come and see them!"

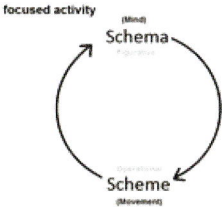

Having introduced the letters with their sounds to Flora, her key person later played a game of 'find the letter', *"Where is the letter 'f'? Can you find the letter 'o'? Can you trace over the letter 'o'? Can you trace the letter 'l'?"* Flora followed all the instructions and laughed throughout the activity, smiling every time she identified a letter correctly (an adaptation of a Montessori 'three-period lesson').

When the game had finished, Flora said:

"Again, let's, can we, play again?"

A few days later her key person encouraged Flora to play a game where she listened to the sounds of each letter in her name and she was asked to find the letter that matched the sound and to place it on a table and then to trace it (virtually writing her own name).

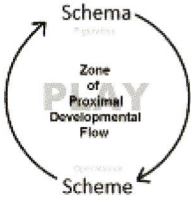

A week later Flora was observed sitting on a mat in her free -flow play. She was playing with two small world objects (a dog and a cat) and a collection of card letters that she had made. Flora said to herself:

"What sound can I hear first? d, d, d, d-o-g; d".

She traced her fingers over the letter 'd', smiled and placed it' alongside the dog. She then said, "d/o, d/o, d/o. 'o' is in my name". She traced 'o' on the card and then sat back to look at the letters she had selected so far. Then she said:

"g', 'd', 'o', 'g'; I made dog".

Flora traced over all three letters using her left index and middle fingers and then selected a picture showing fog. Flora carried out the same process of saying the letter sound and finding the appropriate letters to write 'fog'.

In her free-flow play, Flora started to make some words out of the letters she has made. Identifying the first, middle and end sounds in each word. Objects were provided to help her consider the sounds in the nouns. She traced over the letters she had made and placed them in position. The activity of saying the letter sound and finding the appropriate letter had been introduced to Flora only two days previously and this was the first time her key person had ever seen her choosing to play with letters in her free-flow play.

It was decided that the letters should be available on the shelf at all times after that and, once it appeared that Flora had finished making the words chosen, some new small world animals were added to the basket next to where the letters were stored. More mark making materials, books and letters were also added in different areas of the classroom including the role-play area, to 'seed' Flora's playful learning further.

In January 2017, Flora was 3 years and 11 months old and we received a note from Rachael, her key person:

*"I had to share an exciting observation that I recorded today, Flora built six words in her free flow play using the sandpaper letters."*

The following day Rachael wrote again:

*"Flora has asked me if we could sound out the letters in*

*'Mummy'. She was holding a pencil and paper and gestured to me to sit at a table next to her. As we sounded out the letters m/u/m, Flora wrote the word 'mum'. She did this twice and then put her own name on the top of her paper! I cannot believe that she has drawn together the schemes, just as we discussed in the training, and is now writing words!"*

27/1/17

F L O

MOM

MUM

In observing Flora over a period of three months we identified each of the following schemes being applied in finally supporting her emergent writing (see chapter 4):

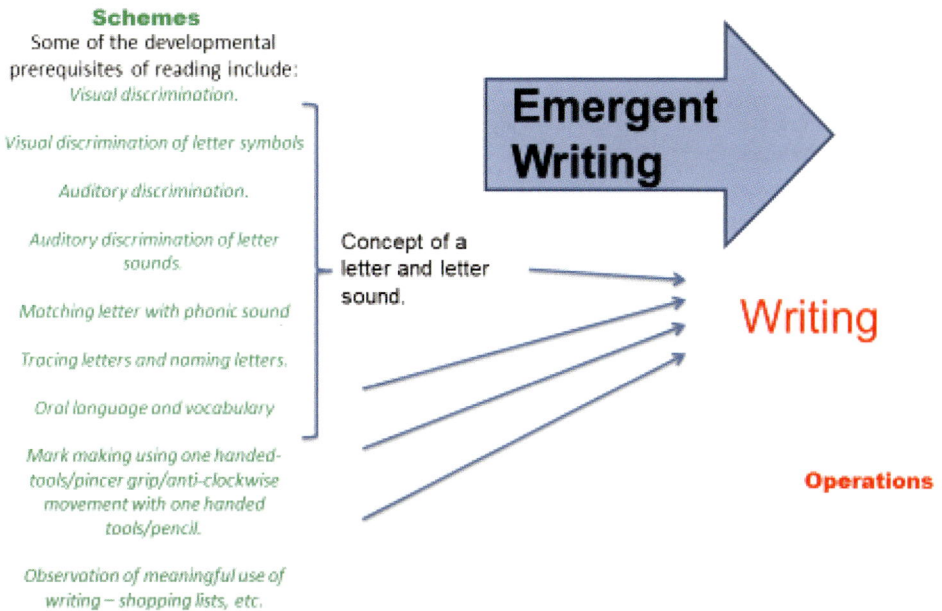

**Schemes**
Some of the developmental prerequisites of reading include:
*Visual discrimination.*

*Visual discrimination of letter symbols*

*Auditory discrimination.*

*Auditory discrimination of letter sounds.*

*Matching letter with phonic sound*

*Tracing letters and naming letters.*

*Oral language and vocabulary*

*Mark making using one handed-tools/pincer grip/anti-clockwise movement with one handed tools/pencil.*

*Observation of meaningful use of writing – shopping lists, etc.*

Concept of a letter and letter sound.

**Emergent Writing**

Writing

**Operations**

**An Emergent Curriculum** recognises that the sophisticated cognitive operations that emerge in children are irreducible to their component parts, which nevertheless act as developmental precursors that must be drawn together in the child's mind as a unique and individual creative act.

**Fiona (3:5)** attended the same pre-school in Kent and was first observed by us in November 2016 playing in the role-play area. There were other children in the area, who Fiona acknowledged from time to time by looking at them, or with a response to something that they said, but generally she was totally immersed in her socio-dramatic play of 'cooking dinner'.

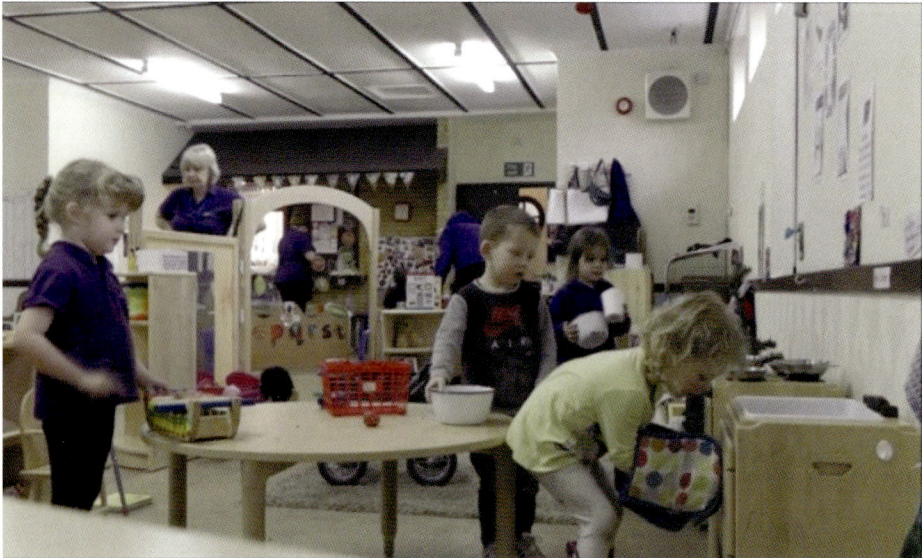

She said aloud:

*"This is going to be a big casserole."*

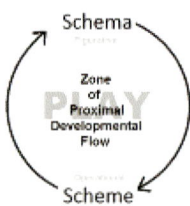

She mixed plastic 'pretend' vegetables around in a pot then, put on a pair of oven gloves, picked up the pot and placed it inside a toy oven. She crouched down to look through the door, then turned the dial on the oven and stood up saying:

*"That should do it!"*

She then picked up some other pretend food and said to herself:

*"So much washing!"*

She then walked over to a sophisticated toy washing machine, placed the food inside and then pressed a button which made the drum rotate. She crouched down to watch the food going around in the drum.

It was decided that a variety of resources, both indoors and outdoors, should be provided to seed and support her enclosing scheme; these included cupboards with different opening mechanisms, bags, etc.

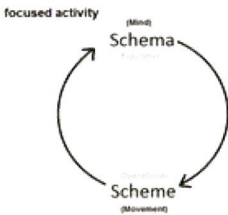

Building upon the enclosing scheme, it was also suggested that Fiona might be introduced to a sorting game, which included enclosing objects. She was introduced to an egg box activity that involved sorting different sizes of toy eggs where the large eggs would only fit into the sockets in one of the boxes, the medium size ones would fit in to the sockets of two boxes and the smallest eggs could potentially fit into the sockets of all three boxes.

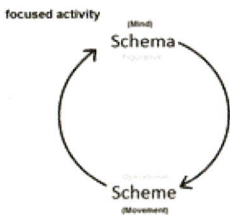

A clothes sorting activity was also introduced to her; involving her sorting clothes by colour, which she could then place inside the washing machine and 'wash' together, finally pairing up the colours on a washing line. This activity was introduced to Fiona to try and extend upon her use of the enclosing scheme as well as to further develop her matching scheme.

Fiona's key person was also keen to identify whether her enclosing and rotating schemes were being applied in any other activities and play themes.

27

Schema

Zone of Proximal Developmental Flow

Scheme

Four days later Fiona's key person advised that she had re-visited the eggs sorting by size activity in her free-flow play every day. She was then observed in her free-flow play, taking all of the eggs out of the boxes and placing them on a table. She selected one of the boxes and returned the eggs. Then she announced:

*"Oh, these eggs can be opened up – look."*

Fiona opened up six egg halves and put them back together again. She then opened up the large egg box and walked over to a chair where she sat with the box on her lap and spent ten minutes opening up the eggs, putting them back together again and then returning them to their sockets in the egg box. As she returned the box to a shelf, she turned to a friend and said:

"I fitted the big eggs together and put them inside here."

The boy responded by asking if she had done the little eggs. Fiona nodded and replied:

"I already didded them and put them over there!"

# Chapter Four

# Emergence and the EYFS curriculum

In previous chapters, we have explained how free-flow play 'works'; how it provides children with the freedom to explore and try out their newly acquired skills knowledge and capabilities, in a variety of new contexts. It is in the process of 'hands on' free-flow play that children first make the sort of connections in their minds that will later increasingly be made through abstract reflection. In Piagetian terms, free-flow play provides a crucially important opportunity for children to assimilate newly acquired operative schemes within existing figurative schemas; and to apply new schemas to schemes.

In the earliest years most of children's newly acquired schemes and schemas come through observation and imitation, they learn most of their new actions and behaviours from the significant adults and children around them. But as children's learning and development advances, focussed learning activities become more significant. Many preschools underestimate the amount of focussed learning interactions that adults provide, but one only needs to consider the priorities that are given to hygiene practices, social interactions, safety, rules, routines and order to appreciate that it is common practice. There are, however, controversies surrounding the extent to which formal learning activities should be provided in preschools to support children's academic learning and development, and;

… clearly it isn't sufficient to say that if a child is capable of learning something at a particular age then we should teach them. If that were true, we might see every two-year-old playing the violin!

In a Montessori environment, focused learning activities are systematically introduced to each child, during the sensitive periods, and at a time that they are observed to have an interest, and have reached an appropriate stage in their development where they will benefit from them. Montessori educators put children in contact with new materials/focussed activities on a daily basis; but the children are also provided with three hours of uninterrupted free-flow play time in which they freely access the materials that have been introduced to them and apply their new schemes and schemas. There are other preschools who take pride in offering children almost complete freedom of play without interruption, while most preschools compromise and offer varied proportions of focused instruction, and free play.

There are two major justifications for including some degree of focused activities in preschools and they are both supported by significant research evidence and academic authority:

As Montessori (2013) observed over a century ago; child development passes through 'sensitive periods' for language (0-72 months), order (12-36 months), sensory skills (0-48 months), motor skills (18-48 months) and social skills (30-72 months).

Today, many psychologists and neuroscientists have identified similar periods of special sensitivity to environmental stimulation and instruction. While learning in these areas may be possible throughout the learning life-course, it is felt that any lack of appropriate provision during these crucial periods could mean that significant opportunities for learning and development are missed. Second language acquisition is widely held to be more effective in childhood.

## 'Sensitive periods' in early brain development

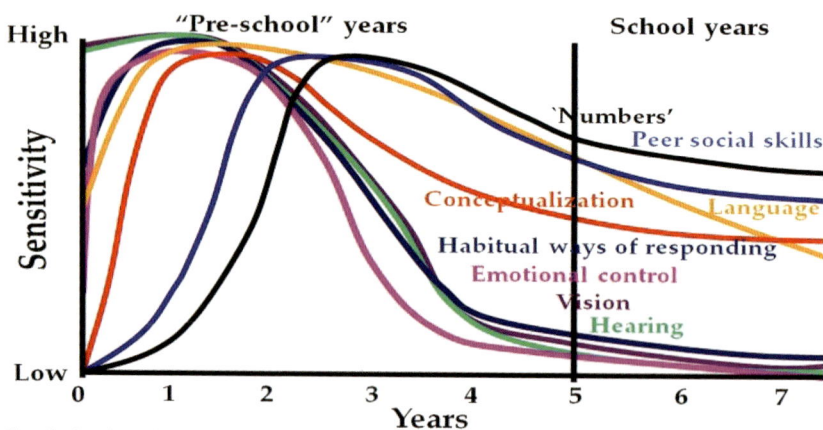

Graph developed by Council for Early Child Development (ref: Nash, 1997; Early Years Study, 1999; Shonkoff, 2000.)

Children's early attachment and language needs are also widely recognised, other areas of particular relevance to preschools have been identified by Nash (1997) and Shonkoff (2000).

The most significant reason that policy makers have cited in support of increased 'teaching' in the English Early Years Foundation Stage (EYFS) (DfE, 2014) in recent years has been related to social justice and equality. Research evidence has shown that some balance between teacher initiated learning activities and free play in preschools can significantly compensate for early learning and developmental disadvantage with at least the potential of creating a 'level playing field' for most children entering school at age 5 (Sylva et al, 2010). From this perspective, investments such as *Every Child a Reader* and *SureStart* are directly addressing the moral and economic imperatives to intervene in the intergenerational processes that reproduce poverty (in material and aspirational terms), and also to address human and children's rights concerns associated with the systematic underachievement of individual children due to what may be considered merely an 'accident of birth'.

One issue that has been highlighted more than any other in the context of discussions about the use of teacher-led focused activities in the EYFS has been the issue of supporting children's reading, and the introduction of focused activities related to phonics. Children benefit from learning to recognise the letter sounds associated with letter symbols, but it is also important to recognise that, however well they are taught, learning phonics will not be sufficient to enable a child to read. Oral language development is crucially important.

When we read, we do not use letter sounds to decode every word, in fact researchers studying eye movements have shown that we do not even look at most of the words in a text when we read. We skip over 15% of all the content words (nouns, verbs, adjectives and adverbs) and 65% of all the function words (prepositions, conjunctions, articles and pronouns) (Paulson and Freeman, 2003). Most literacy experts advocate an 'emergent' approach to literacy education that recognises the importance of oral language development, and stress the importance of focused activities such as reading a range of different kinds of text to children, drawing their attention to the value and uses of text in the world around them, as well as phonics.

Children need to develop the concept of what a book is before they read. The various orientation and direction of scanning the textual characters of a language must be learnt as well as the letter sounds, and all of these provide different skills supporting the accomplishment of reading. Teacher initiated focused activities are provided in most preschools to support the children in developing all of these prerequisite schemes. Playful 'mark making' is therefore encouraged as a natural prelude to writing as we discussed in the context of Flora's learning journey in chapter 3.

'Emergent Literacy' was in fact, a term first applied in Marie Clay's doctoral dissertation (Clay, 1966), and Sulzby and Teale (1991) define the concept as:

"…the skills, knowledge, and attitudes that are presumed to be developmental precursors to conventional forms of reading and writing", as well as; "…the environments that support these developments." (p. 849).

'Emergence' is a philosophical notion that dates back to the earliest writings in 19th Century psychology, and an underlying assumption in the developmental psychologies of both Piaget and Vygotsky (Sawyer, 2003). When the term is applied to early childhood learning and development it suggests that the cognitive structures that emerge in children are not determined, and cannot be reduced to their component parts.

Emergence as a natural phenomenon has been found in many complex systems, and in chemistry we might consider the simple example of a water molecule which has numerous properties that are entirely absent in the hydrogen and oxygen that makes it up. The practical implications of 'emergence' in education is that we cannot break down any complex operation or concept into its component parts and teach each separately, and then expect the child to automatically understand the whole.

All of the component schemes and schema may be in place (all the concepts, attitudes and understandings) and yet the child may still not be able to carry out a complex operation (reading, addition for example), until they are motivated and prepared to develop (for themselves spontaneously) the higher order scheme/schema that brings together all of the prerequisite schemes and schemas for reading. Learning is at the most fundamental level, an individual, and a creative act.

The concept of an 'Emergent Curriculum' has been applied to practices and resources being used to support young children in learning the skills, knowledge and attitudes identified as developmental precursors to a much wider range of curriculum subject areas. Whitebread (1995) argued for an emergent mathematics education, and Siraj-Blatchford (2000) and Siraj-Blatchford and Whitebread, (2003) have also written about an Emergent Science and Technology Education. In our training we provide support in developing a greater awareness of a range of significant prerequisite schemes and have developed a common format for presenting them.

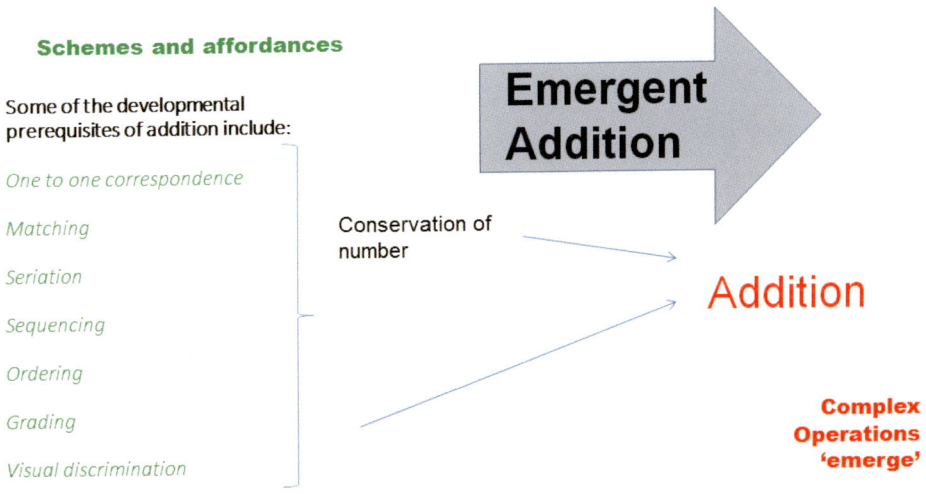

**Schemes and affordances**

Some of the developmental prerequisites of addition include:

*One to one correspondence*

*Matching*

*Seriation*

*Sequencing*

*Ordering*

*Grading*

*Visual discrimination*

Conservation of number

**Emergent Addition**

Addition

**Complex Operations 'emerge'**

*An Emergent Curriculum recognises that the sophisticated cognitive operations that emerge in children are irreducible to their component parts, which nevertheless act as developmental precursors that must be drawn together in the child's mind as a unique and individual creative act.*

## Emergent Education for Sustainable Citizenship

We are currently working in partnership with Kent County Council Early Years and Child Care Service applying the SchemaPlay ZPDF model in the establishment of an emergent curriculum for Education for Sustainable Citizenship (ESC). This is a collaborative project and has involved six preschools in running trials and exemplar practices for dissemination across the county. News of the project will be regularly posted on our website at:

http://www.schemaplay.com

Literature reviews, and an analysis of a wide range of documents including the Earth Charter (2000), have been carried out to identify some of the key developmental prerequisites for sustainable citizenship.

**Prerequisites**

*Independence*

*Making choices*

*Recognising feeling states*     Empathy

*Mutual respect and conflict resolution*

*Identity, ethnicity*     Rights and responsibilities

*Taking risks and responsibility for themselves and others (including animals and the environment)*

*Animal species*     Interdependence

*Global geographic and environmental features*

*Deep engagement with environment*

**Emergence**

**Sustainable Citizenship**

**'...an emergent life-long learning achievement'**

Montessori's (1949) 'cosmic' educational is extremely relevant to ESC in early childhood, and her perspective emphasised the importance of recognising the interdependency between the peoples of the world, and between humanity and natural world:

34

"The trees that purify the air, the herbs that capture vitamins from sunlight, the coral that filters the sea, which teems with countless creatures that would die if there were no such forms of life to keep the water pure, the animals that populate the earth are unconscious of their cosmic mission, but without them the harmony of creation would not exist and life would cease." (Montessori, 1949, footnote p117)

Focused activities, including many sourced 'off the shelf' from Montessori 'cosmic' education resources are being developed to provide the children with appropriate schemes that they may apply in their free play and in support of their emergent sustainable citizenship. There are many general features of Montessori practice that support this initiative. Research suggests that the Montessori emphasis on children developing their independence, and in support of 'grace and courtesy' support the development of empathy. There are also activities focused on developing the child's 'cosmic' or holistic understanding of the world they inhabit. These include activities and games focused on the Sun and food chains, land and water forms, the continents, animal families and the classification of the animal kingdom, life cycles, and natural habitats. New focused activities are also being developed to supplement these. For more information see Siraj-Blatchford and Brock (2016) and look out for the next booklet in this series to be published later this year:

Siraj-Blatchford, J., and Brock, L. (forthcoming 2017) *Education for Sustainable Citizenship in Early Childhood, SchemaPlay Publications*

Children learn about food chains, and interdependence and ecology as they play with the Sun Game

A 'Nursery in a Nursery'; learning about the green economy as children grow hyacinths for sale at Christmas

# References

Alexander, R. (Ed.) (2010) *Children, their world, their education: Final report and recommendations of the Cambridge Primary Review*, Routledge

Anderson, R.C. and Spiro, J. (Eds.) (1977) *Schooling and the Acquisition of Knowledge*. USA: Lawrence Erlbaum

Athey, C, (1990; 2007) *Extending Thought in Young Children*, London: Sage Publications

Bodrova, E. and Leong, D.J. (2007) *Tools of the Mind*, New Jersey: Pearson Education Inc.

Bruce, T. (2004) 'Play Matters' in L. Abbot, and A. Langston, (eds) *Birth to Three Matters: supporting the framework of effective practice*, Open University Press: Maidenhead

Clay, M. M. (1966*) Emergent reading behavior*. Unpublished doctoral dissertation, University of Auckland, New Zealand.

Csikszentmihalyi, M. (1990) *Flow: The Psychology of Optimal Experience*, New York: Harper & Row

Department for Education (2013) *Early Years Outcomes: A non-statutory guide for practitioners and inspectors to help inform understanding of child development through the early years, England*, Retrieved from: http://www.foundationyears.org.uk/files/2012/03/early_years_outcomes.pdf

Department for Education (2014) *Statutory framework for the early years foundation stage: Setting the standards for learning, development and care for children from birth to five, England*, Retrieved from: https://www.gov.uk/government/uploads/system/uploads/attachment_data/file/335504/EYFS_framework_from_1_September_2014__with_clarification_note.pdf

Fagard, J. Wolff, P. (1991) *The Development of Timing Control and Temporal Organization in Coordinated Action*, Amsterdam: Elsevier Fmont

Furth, H.G. (1969) *Piaget and Knowledge: Theoretical Foundation*, USA: Prentice-Hall

Gibson, E.J. (1969) *Principles of perceptual learning and development*, New York: Meredith Corporation

Laevers, F. (1993) Deep level learning: An exemplary application on the area of physical knowledge. *European Early Childhood Education Research Journal*, 1 (1), pp 53-68

Montessori, M. (1949: 1992) *Education and Peace:* The Clio Montessori Series, Oxford, Clio Press

Montessori, M. (2012) The 1946 London Lectures*, Amsterdam: Montessori Pierson Publishing*

Montessori, M. (2013) *The Absorbent Mind*, USA: Start Publishing LLC

Nash, M. (1997) "How a Child's Brain Develops." *Time* 3 February: pp48- 56

Neisser, U. (1976) *Cognition & Reality*, San Francisco: Freeman

Nutbrown, C. (2006) *Threads of Thinking,* London: SAGE Publications Ltd

Paulson, E. and Freeman, A. (2003) *Insight from the eyes: The science of effective reading instruction.* NH: Heinemann.

Piaget, J. (1962) *Play, Dreams and Imitation in Childhood,* New York: Norton & Company

Piaget, J. (1969) *The Mechanisms of Perception*, New York: Basic Books

Rogoff, B. (1990) *Apprenticeship in thinking: Cognitive development in social context.* New York: Oxford University Press.

Sawyer, R. (2003) Emergence in creativity and development, In R. Sawyer, V. John-Steiner, S. Moran, & D. Feldman, *Creativity & Development*, Oxford, England: Oxford University Press.

Shonkoff, J.P. (2000) Science, policy, and practice: Three cultures in search of a shared mission. *Child Development* 71(1): pp181-187.

Siraj-Blatchford, J. (2000) Emergent Science, in F. McKeon (Ed.) *SciCentre 2000, and ASET Conference Report, National Centre for Initial Teacher Training in Primary School Science*

Siraj-Blatchford, J. (2001) Emergent Science and Technology in the Early Years, Paper presented at the *XXIII WORLD CONGRESS OF OMEP, Santiago* Chile, July

Siraj-Blatchford, J., and Brock, L. (2015) Taking play more seriously: A Montessori approach to understanding Free Flow Play, *Research Brief*, presented at TACTYC Conference, Birmingham, November, Retrieved from: http://tactyc.org.uk/wp-content/uploads/2015/10/John-Siraj-Blatchford-and-Lynette-Brock_TakingPlayMoreSeriously.pdf

Siraj-Blatchford, J., and Brock, L. (2016) Wellbeing and Sustainable Development: The legacy of Maria Montessori, paper presented at the *European Early Childhood Education Research (EECERA) Conference,* Dublin, September access at: http://www.schemaplay.com/Docs/Wellbeing_SD.pdf

Siraj-Blatchford, J. and Whitebread, D. (2003) *Supporting ICT in the Early Years*, UK, McGraw-Hill Education

Sulzby, E., & Teale, W. (1991). Emergent literacy, in R. Barr, M. Kamil, P. Mosenthal, & P. D. Pearson (Eds.), *Hand-book of reading research* (Vol. 2, pp727-758). New York: Longman.

*The Earth Charter,* Earth Charter International Secretariat (2000), Retrieved from: http://www.earthcharter.org

Van Oers, B. (1999) Teaching Opportunities in Play, in M. Hedegaard, and J. Lompscher (Eds) *Learning Activity and Development,* Aarhus University Press, Aarhus

Vygotsky, L. S. (1962) *Thought and Language.* Cambridge, MA US: MIT Press

Vygotsky, L. S. (1978) *Mind in Society: Development of Higher Psychological Processes,* Cambridge, MA: Harvard University Press

Vygotsky, L. S. (1987) Thinking and Speech in R. W. Rieber (Ed.), *The Collected Works of L. S. Vygotsky*, Vol. 4: The History of the Development of Higher Mental Functions, New York: Plenum Press

Whitebread, D. (1995) Emergent Mathematics or how to help young children become confident mathematicians, in J. Anghileri (Ed.) *Children's Mathematical Thinking in the Primary Years,* England, A&C Black

# Index